Sandeep Jandu

STITCHING
PICTURES

A&C Black • London

A&C Black, London
First published in Great Britain 2012
A&C Black Publishers
an imprint of Bloomsbury Publishing Plc
50 Bedford Square
London
WC1B 3DP

ISBN: 9781408131343

A CIP catalogue record for this book is available from the
British Library

Publisher: Susan James
Page design: Evelin Kasikov
Cover design: Sutchinda Thompson
Managing Editor: Davida Saunders
Copy editor: Julie Brooke
Photographs © Hema Patel unless otherwise stated.
Illustrations by Sandeep Jandu.

This book is produced using paper that is made from
wood grown in managed, sustainable forests. It is natural,
renewable and recyclable. The logging and manufacturing
processes conform to the environmental regulations of
the country of origin.

Printed and bound in China.

Everything written in this book is to the best of the author's
knowledge and every effort has been made to ensure
accuracy and safety but neither author nor publisher can be
held responsible for any resulting injury, damage or loss to
either persons or property. Any further information that will
assist in updating of any future editions would be gratefully
received. Read through all the information in each chapter
before commencing work. Follow all health and safety
guidelines and where necessary obtain health and safety
information from the suppliers. Health and Safety information
can also be found on the internet about certain products.

CONTENTS

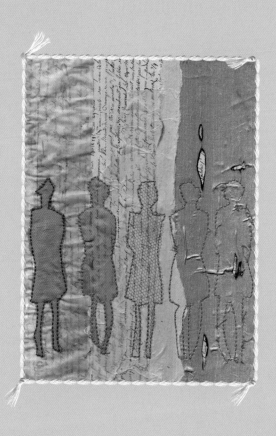

Acknowledgements

I would like to thank all of the featured artists for their generosity in sharing their work and making this book a truly inspirational resource. Without Hema Patel and Evelin Kasikov this book would not have looked as beautiful as it does, so thank you.

I would also like to thank Jane Stobart, my illustration tutor at university for her continuous support and encouragement; without her I would not have developed the skills and creativity that led me to the opportunity to make this book.

My artwork would have never been created with such passion without the inspiration I gained from my Grandma when I was a little girl – a special thank you to her for always letting me experiment with her sewing machine. A big thank you to my mum for doing last-minute craft shop runs during my projects! (And putting up with having paint, thread and paper all around the house).

And finally, thank you to Susan James for making this book a possibility and to Davida Saunders for her extensive support, guidance and patience – I could not have completed this book without you.

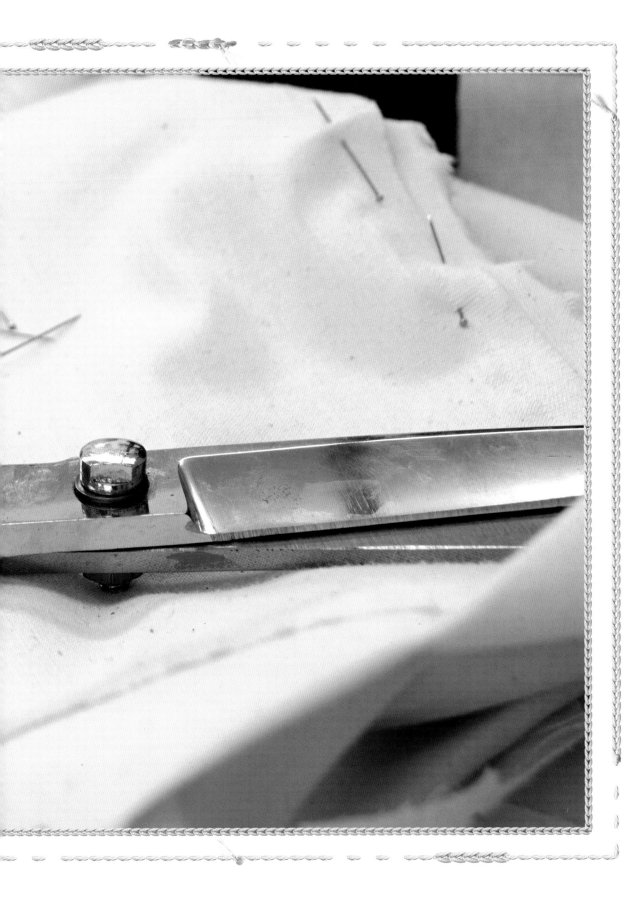

INTRODUCTION

Textile design, and mixed-media techniques that combine textiles with needlework, paper and print, are often overlooked as an art form. For many these pieces are also difficult to categorise as examples of either fine art or craft. Even so, fashion designers, contemporary artists and interior designers all combine fabrics, paper, patterns, threads and embellishments to create varied works of art.

There are many books that explain traditional stitching methods, how to knit, print and other handcraft techniques. These skills are undergoing a revival today as people return to traditional crafts and find new ways to apply them. I am a mixed-media and textile artist, creating images and backgrounds by combining everyday materials and fabrics with threads and sewing machine stitches. I specialised in illustration in my degree, but straight away I was influenced by fashion designers, embroiderers, appliqué artists, fabric designers and others working in mixed media, rather than in ink on paper. My aim is to shift the emphasis away from precise craft techniques and on to imaginative ways to combine materials and techniques, often using practices that are centuries old. For example, I use delicate needlework, machine stitch and chunky hand stitch to create illustrations, rather than the traditional lines drawn with pen and ink.

Thanks to my Indian background, and particularly the influence of my grandmother, I was introduced to rich and luxurious fabrics at an early age. My grandmother worked in a tailoring factory for most of her life, and has always sewn the traditional Indian outfits I wear. From a very young age I would sit with her and simply stitch pieces of fabric together. My work continues to echo my early fascination with textiles. I am particularly interested in the variety of qualities a single piece of fabric has, and the way it can be manipulated and juxtaposed with other materials to create different effects. Historically, textile skills such as embroidery, patchwork and appliqué were feminine pastimes and among the few which allowed women to express their creativity. For me, this brings deeper levels of meaning to textile art and has become a key aspect of my work. It is this personal and subtle approach that I wish to convey through the tactile surface of the fabric. Experimentation is just as important as process. Texture, aesthetics and trying out different media have become the most important aspects of my own work and I hope you will enjoy this too. Personally, this approach has allowed me to develop my illustrations, so that they have become individual pieces of art that demonstrate the process of construction while simultaneously rendered as small, precious 'keepsakes'

Artists are free to be inspired by a wide range of people: Vivienne Westwood is an obvious influence in my work. High fashion is an incredible industry, creating exquisitely crafted clothes in beautiful fabrics that are pieced together with gorgeous hand-embroidery and embellished with intricate detailing. These creations are true works of art, which help to clarify the relationship between fine art and textiles.

These couture garments inspire similar designs from/high street retailers who then make them available to the mass-market. In this way, more and more people are coming to appreciate the unique nature of mixed-media and embroidered textiles which can be seen in home furnishings, gift shops and designer diffusion lines such as that created by Matthew Williamson for Debenhams, which in turn has made him a household name.

I also admire innovative contemporary artists such as Kathyrn McDonald, Sammy-Jane Kenny, Cos Ahmet, Georgie Meadows and Seainin Passi, who have each been kind enough to contribute illustrations and projects in this book. I hope that you will be as inspired by their work as I am.

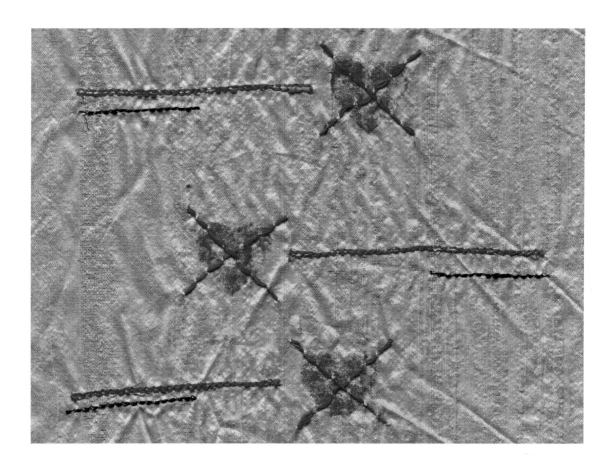

MAKING THE MOST OF THIS BOOK

Before you begin, flick through the book and decide which techniques and effects you'd like to explore or combine. This book features a number of mixed-media projects and explores a new kind of drawing and image-making. The projects will allow you to experiment with paint, collage, watercolours, wax, stencils and mono print techniques, thereby developing your own style. They also break some of the boundaries surrounding traditional skills such as embroidery. These projects offer a contemporary approach to these conventional methods of 'drawing', and new ways to apply lines to create artwork and dramatic visual effects. The projects are suitable for all skill levels but there's plenty of scope for advanced artists to incorporate more complex techniques.

The complexity of the projects varies, but each one aims to unlock your passion for mixed media and develop your creativity. They highlight the wide range of qualities a single fabric can offer, and set out different ways to use fabrics to create different effects. I hope that the projects in this book communicate my passion, creativity and desire to create original designs inspired by the combination of different media.

When following the projects, allow yourself to be captivated by the magic of experimentation, as well as mistake. Enjoy yourself!

Tools

For most of the projects included in this book you will need the following tools.

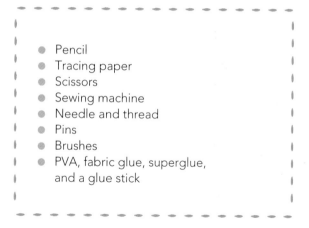

- Pencil
- Tracing paper
- Scissors
- Sewing machine
- Needle and thread
- Pins
- Brushes
- PVA, fabric glue, superglue, and a glue stick

Some projects in this book may require a more specific piece of equipment to complete a desired finish or technique, and these are listed as part of the project.

1

Materials

TIP ❯ Have confidence in your fabric decisions and choose bold or unexpected combinations of textures and colours.

TIP ❯ There is no limit to the way materials can be manipulated to create an interesting work of art. Remember that when creating a mixed-media image you may develop a style or technique by 'mistake', and inspiration for a new material can be found in the simplest places, such as your kitchen; you may, for example, try using non-stick baking paper in your artwork.

Whether I choose torn fabric, or fabric with shredded selvedges, hand-stitched or unpicked embroidery threads, my aim is to translate pencil drawings into textile designs using images, mixed-media and print. There are no limitations when it comes to choosing materials for a piece of mixed-media artwork, so do not be afraid to try new combinations. For example, I often find that a combination of man-made and natural fabrics creates the most interesting and complex finishes.

Before attempting the projects in this book you should start building a collection of aesthetically pleasing fabrics and objects which you can incorporate into your artwork, for example old jeans, packaging and safety pins. Push the boundaries – don't just collect the obvious materials (see 'Found objects' on p.21).

Photograph ©: Larina Natalia

Detail from Hansel and Gretel project (see p.50).

TIP ❯ Beads and buttons are a simple but beautiful way to add intricate design features to your artwork.

Detail from wall hanging by Sammy-Jane Kenny (see p.108).

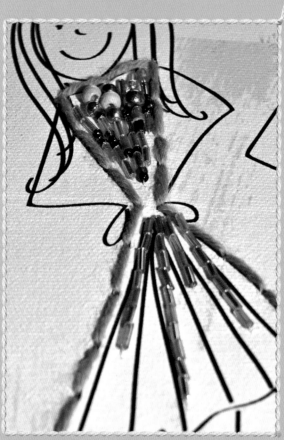

Detail from wall hanging by Sammy-Jane Kenny (see p.108).

TEXTILES

My creative passion for textile illustration has led me to explore an extensive range of fabrics. I want to discover the many qualities that each different material has, whether it is a unique sheen, texture, malleability or other characteristic, and learn how each material can be manipulated alone or with others to create a work of art.

Techniques you can use with textiles include including printing, appliqué, embroidery and collage, and different types of fabric will yield different results, bringing a different finish and feel to an artwork. For example, you may want to use plain yarn materials such as cotton or calico for backgrounds, felt for bold, colourful pieces and silks for intricate designs. Embroidery and other threads and ribbon can be incorporated into an artwork to introduce additional textures in a minimal way.

Photograph © Vovan

PAPER

Paper is often overlooked as a material, or artists limit themselves to plain white or coloured sheets, which is a shame because it's a versatile and inexpensive material. Think like a mixed-media artist and source paper from found objects such as old textbooks, newspapers, wallpaper or packaging; use handmade paper to create interesting finishes; or try tissue paper to build up layers.

The delicate nature of paper makes it is easy to manipulate to produce interesting – often unexpected – surfaces. For example, try colouring it by coffee- or tea-staining (see p.46–7). Dunking paper into strong tea or coffee (without milk) is a quick and simple way to add colour. If you want to take this further you could also experiment with dyes – follow the instructions on the packaging.

Don't just stick to 'ordinary' paper. Try working with the following:

Baking paper

Note: baking paper is specifically treated to withstand heat. Don't try this with other types of papers.

When baking paper is placed inside an oven on a low heat it will crinkle to create interesting effects.

Handmade paper

You can experiment making your own paper; process similar to making papier-mâché – so simple! This can produce interesting and unexpected surfaces. Handmade paper is easy to make and has a unique finish every time.

- Select pieces of paper to use as your materials. These can range from tissue paper to newspaper and can be different colours.

- Wrap a piece of cling film over a square of cardboard a little large than the paper sheet you want to make, keeping it taught.

- Apply PVA glue over the cling film and the arrange the desired pieces of paper as you wish.

- Keep repeating the process until you have achieved your desired effect.

- Leave to dry and then peel the paper from the cling film.

Try introducing leaves, flowers and other embellishments to your paper. This works best with thin paper like tissue paper as your base layer.

- Apply a layer of PVA glue to cling film and then a layer of thin fabric.

- Arrange your decoration on top of the fabric, and then glue another layer of paper on top.

- Complete with another layer of glue and leave to dry.

Heavy paper or card

Try working with paper or card that is tough enough to withstand strong surface treatments without disintegrating. Try scratching, burning, layering and painting.

TIP ❯ It is exciting to look beyond a material's traditional qualities, such as colour, texture etc, and explore its boundaries. Don't be scared to try tearing, cutting, burning, layering to see what happens. Try these techniques with different weights of fabric, such as denim, silk and net.

PHOTOGRAPHS AND PRINTED IMAGES

Photographs and printed images are ideal collage or background materials. They can be manipulated by scratching, tearing or printing on top of them and are relatively inexpensive to use.

I have always found fashion magazines inspirational – I tear out my favourite pages to use in my work. You may want to collect cuttings as well as other things such as maps, invitations and vintage posters as starting points to use in your work, and even make them part of a design.

TIP ❯ You may find you are inspired by examples of interesting lettering. Or try tearing out phrases from a newspaper or magazine, using these to inspire a design.

TIP There are many ways to apply the paint to your material. If you don't want to use a traditional brush, try experimenting with cardboard. This technique is very effective and easy to do: simply dip a scrap of cardboard big enough to hold comfortably into the paint and wipe it over your surface. For an interesting finished effect, explore mixing paints directly on your fabric.

PAINT

Paint is a simple material that is frequently used in mixed-media artwork. There are many types to choose from, including acrylic, watercolour, household emulsion and printing inks and dye. Paint can be used as a prominent material or as a finish or manipulation technique. The projects in this book mainly use acrylic or emulsion paints and, just like the materials, it is important to research how a particular paint will work for your project. For example, oil paints take a long time to dry, so layering would not work, unless you have a lot of spare time!

FOUND OBJECTS

As you explore the projects in this book, and find inspiration, you will begin to collect a range of found objects. They are often the most exciting materials with which to work. Look for ways in which you can combine different textures and colours to create interesting contrasts. Found objects can include anything, from discarded packaging, to safety pins, to clothing labels and old jewellery. You may want to incorporate something personal in your work, for example, shells you on the beach while on holiday. These will help to bring a story into your piece. (See p.109 for more ideas.) Anything can be included in your work – just make and experiment!

2

Colour

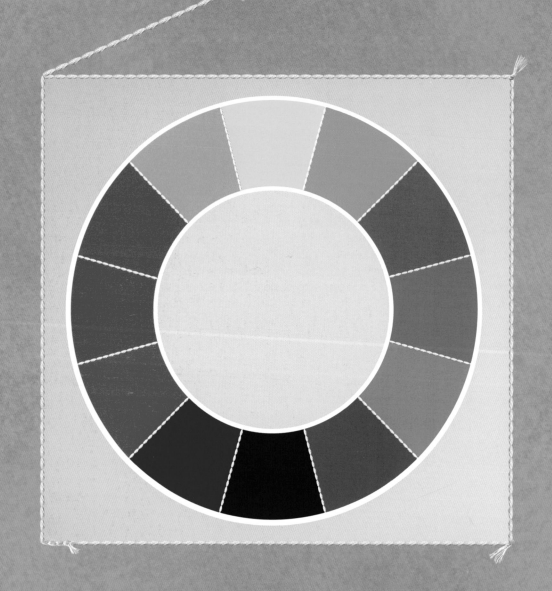

Colour theory is a large area of study that encompasses many concepts. As a creative, you may already have an eye for how you wish to combine certain shades, but if you are new to mixed-media art you may want to take inspiration from the simple ideas abut how to use colour below.

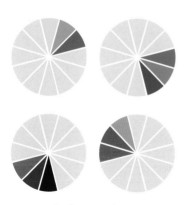

Analogous colours

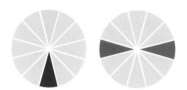

Complementary colours

Analogous colours

These are three colours that sit side-by-side on the colour wheel, such as yellow-green, yellow and yellow-orange. You could use a simple tonal palette of analogous colours for your colour scheme. Usually, one colour predominates and this could be used as your background colour.

Complementary colours

These are two colours that lie directly opposite each other on the wheel, for example, red and green. They create maximum contrast when paired together. You may wish to add a complementary colour to break up the harmony.

Colour schemes

You might want to choose a colour scheme based on a particular theme, for example, natural colours found at the beach, or in the woods at autumn.

Colour Aphothecary by Seainin Passi, linen, wool, cotton, silk and glass jars. Seainin's work is influenced by colour and heritage. This project, part of an installation, was inspired by theories about colour healing. © Royal College of Art / Photograph: Dominic Tschudin.

Other properties of colour to consider:

- *Hue*, the name given to a colour, such as red. Try using the same hue but different shades – for example ruby red and scarlet red.

- *Intensity* or *saturation*, the strength and vividness of a colour as it appears on a given material. For example, the same red dye will look different on tissue paper compared with cotton.

- *Brightness*, the perceived intensity of a colour. A bright green in sunlight does have the same brightness in shade. You can achieve an effect that mimics brightness when using paints or inks by adding black or white to create a tint.

Neutrals

Neutral shades are a simple way to add a calm, sophisticated finish to your artwork. Stronger colours such as primaries can be introduced into neutral schemes successfully, but be careful not to use too many, or too much, with a highly textured and patterned design. Keep blocks of bright colours simple and embellish with tiny details such as hand stitching and beads.

PATTERN

Be careful not to overpower beautiful patterns and fabrics. Intricate designs should be given space to 'breathe' – consider using them as 'stand alone' features in your work. Also remember that too many vibrant colours or bold designs can be distracting and reduce the beauty of your composition. However, patterns such as stripes work well with other designs, especially spots – for good results keep the colours in the same palette. A floral fabric against an antique nude affect always creates a traditional feel.

3

Techniques

Successful one-piece mixed-media works require creativity, originality and imagination. And there is no limit to the techniques and processes you can use to manipulate your materials. Here are the basic techniques you will need.

MACHINE STITCH

Sewing machines have a variety of stitches that can easily be used to create patterns and simple lines. Standard sewing machine stitches include straight, stretch, hem and zigzag stitches. More advanced models will have additional stitches. If you are using the stitch as detailing try setting the machine to make a double stitch – some machines allow four to five stitches wide. A thicker stitch will create a more defined line, which is useful for creating outlines or inserting detail in your work.

TIP ❯ A zigzag stitch is a simple decorative stitch that can be used to create a border, or to add detail to the outline of a particular area of your artwork.

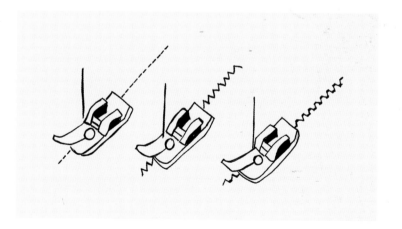

Useful sewing machine notes

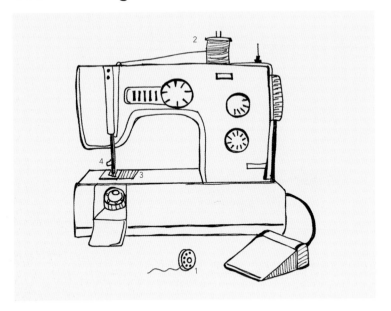

TIP ⋗ To learn how to use any feature on your sewing machine, the machine's manual is the best resource.

Bobbin

The bobbin (1) is a reel of thread that spools underneath the fabric. Each machine stitch is made from two threads: the (upper) main thread (2), and the (lower) bobbin thread, which links with the main thread to make each stitch. You can create interesting yet subtle effects by filling the bobbin with a thread colour that contrasts with your main thread.

Feed dog and presser foot

The feed dog (3) sits under the fabric when it is on the machine and moves it forwards and backwards as you stitch. The presser foot (4) holds the fabric securely against the feed dog and helps to guide the needle.

The feed dog can be positioned up or down. In the 'up' position the fabric passes under the needle in one direction to help to sew straight seams. When lowered or 'dropped' (called a 'drop feed'), it allows the material to be moved in any direction to allow for free machine stitching, such as embroidery, and to achieve the 'free' stitch detail shown in some of the projects in this book.

Fabric chalk

If you are not experienced sewing with a machine or by hand, you may wish to draw the outline you want to create with fabric chalk before using free stitch detail. You can then follow the chalk line and rub it out once it has been stitched.

Pinning and tacking

If you plan to use free stitching to appliqué a shape onto the fabric you may find it helpful to pin or tack the shape on to the fabric first.

Free stitching

Free stitching allows you to work in a much more creative and undefined way. To free stitch you need to attach a part called a free arm to your machine. (Not all machines have this option so check your manual.) More advanced machine stitchers will be able to create shapes and follow more intricate designs. The projects in this book don't require you to use free stitch as a technique since a fairly flexible finish can be more simply achieved using a dog feed, changing the stitch style and experimenting by moving the fabric around while stitching.

Free stitch

HAND STITCH

Hand-stitching is very different from machine-stitching as it creates a much more personal and controlled effect. Moreover, hand-stitching is an easy and effective way to create a deliberately rough finish, while adding small details.

Useful hand stitches

Running stitch

This is the simplest hand stitch.

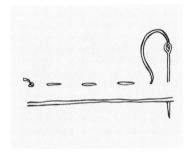

Running stitch

- Tie a knot at the end of the thread, or for a neater effect, fasten the thread with a few stitches on the spot. Bring the needle up from the back of the fabric and pull the thread through until it comes no further. Return the needle through the fabric using a stabbing motion. Continue back and forth through the fabric, working in small stitches. Keep the stitches and spaces as even as possible.

Back stitch

This is the strongest hand stitch and can be used to imitate machine stitching. Backstitch is worked from right to left (although if you are left-handed you may find it easier to work from left to right).

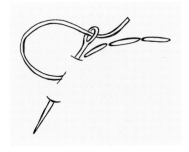

Back stitch

- Begin by working a couple of stitches on the spot, to secure the thread. Then pass the needle through from the front to the back of the fabric and bring the needle through to the right side of the fabric a short distance away from the first stitch to leave a gap.

- Take the needle back over the space, inserting it where it last entered the fabric, to begin the second stitch. Bring it out of the fabric the same distance from the point where it last exited the fabric to begin the third stitch.

- Continue to the end of the seam.

- Fasten off with a couple of stitches on the spot.

Oversewing

This is traditionally used to neaten a raw edge and to prevent fabrics from fraying, but it can also be used as quirky way to add detail to an image.

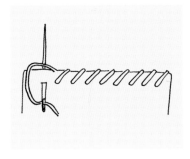

Oversewing

- Begin with a few stitches on the spot to secure the thread.

- Make diagonal stitches over the raw edge, spacing them equally and making them all the same length.

Further stitches

Experienced artists may want to explore simple embroidery techniques such as French knots or cross stitches which can be used to create interesting finishes. Step-by-step instructions on these techniques can be found in specialist embroidery books.

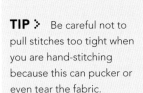

TIP ⸪ Be careful not to pull stitches too tight when you are hand-stitching because this can pucker or even tear the fabric.

MONO PRINT

Basic mono prints are created by drawing or painting on a flat surface and then transferring the design to another surface using pressure. They are unique prints that cannot be exactly recreated. The technique described here is a transfer mono print, where ink is transferred only where pressure is applied. In the picture opposite, the figure of the girl and the text on the right were both created using this technique. It does not require a press but you will need a roller.

Mono prints are ideal as backgrounds and can be simply made using printing ink and scraps of paper.

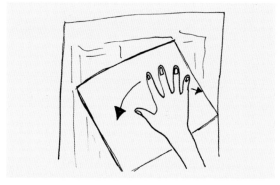

1 Apply printing ink to scrap paper with a print roller. Be sure to achieve good coverage as this will ensure you get a good print.

2 Blot the excess ink with a scrap of paper. The amount left on the paper you will print with will determine the strength of your print. However, too much ink will create an unclear and messy print.

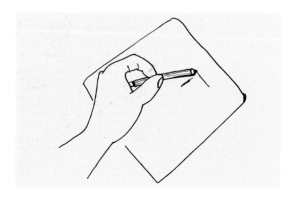

3 Turn the paper ink-face down onto your artwork. Gently draw the image you desire on your fabric on the back of the scrap paper so that it transfers onto the fabric. A pen or pencil is the easiest way to do this.

4 Carefully lift off the paper to reveal your print.

TIP > You may prefer to keep this print simple by following a single outline, as you can use stitching to create contrasting lines later.

TIP > Experiment with different thicknesses of pen or pencil. Try using your fingers to create shading in your print.

APPLIQUÉ

In mixed-media work, appliqué – stitching items onto a background to create an image – is a versatile technique that can be used to give different effects. You can explore traditional methods of appliqué alongside your own experiments, layering a number of different materials on top of each other.

Traditional appliqué usually refers to a technique when one layer of fabric is placed over another and is sewn in place. Simple shapes are usually the simplest for a beginner to use.

- Draw your appliqué design on to a piece plain paper. You may want to divide it into sections and use a different fabric for each one.

- Pin the paper shapes onto the fabric(s) and cut out. Woven cotton fabrics are the easiest to work with, although you may want to experiment with others as you gain experience.

- Pin your fabric shapes in place and then hand- or machine-stitch in place.

COLLAGE

Collage is an ideal technique for mixed-media artworks. A collage is created by layering diverse materials onto a surface. It allows the artists to explore a number of different fabrics and their properties.

The materials you collect for your collage will help to inspire your designs. Both fashion and fine art have been a huge influence in my work – especially beautiful feminine fabrics draped and layered in different ways to create strong silhouettes. I remember all the finely crafted clothes I have seen on catwalks, pieced together in interesting ways and finished with tiny beads and intricate embroidery. I use these ideas to inspire details in my final pieces, while exploring different fabrics.

Try layering different tones, and add texture with contrasting finishes – from glossy photographs to burnt silk – to impart an interesting finish and depth to your work. Using materials with different transparencies is an easy way to create layers in your work. Think about whether you want to tear, rip or use scissors to achieve the desired shape as this will also create a different finish.

TIP ⸬ Use appliqué to add texture to a design. However, when using it to add interest to a background layer, avoid lots of patterns, as these will reduce the impact of the top layer.

TIP ⸬ Inspiration can be found everywhere – from a walk in the countryside to the pages of a magazine. You may want to think about mixing vintage styles with modern ones or decide to make cultural patterns and imagery a starting point. Try to think what is personal to you – this will be a great source of inspiration for your work.

TIP ⸬ There is no need to consistently choose complementary colours – sometimes a harsh or bright colour block can bring a different depth to your collage.

STENCILLING

Stencils are a simple way to reproduce a pattern or design. It is also a great way to add different layers and depth to your work. Experiment with different amounts of paint to create different effects.

You can use stencil brushes to apply the paint; these are short with stiff bristles. Start from the outside of the stencil and work your way in as this will ensure you do not get paint under the outside edges of the stencil. A roller is another way to create the print, though this will produce a much denser image.

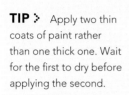

TIP ❯ Apply two thin coats of paint rather than one thick one. Wait for the first to dry before applying the second.

TIP ❯ Practise in your sketchbook before applying the stencil to your final surface.

4

Developing your
ideas

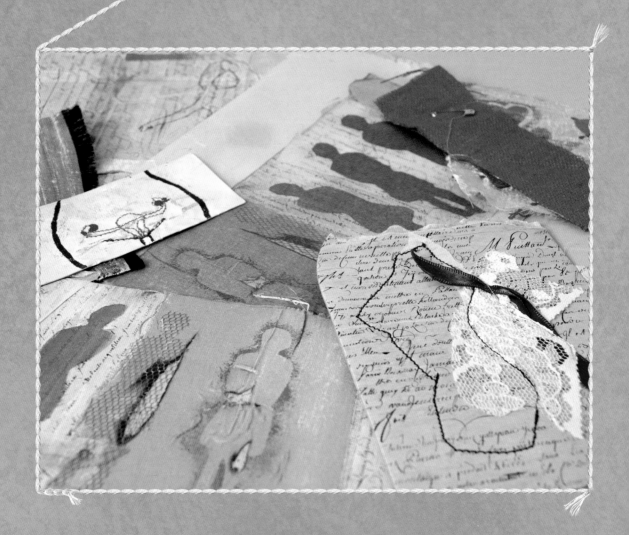

SKETCHBOOKS

A sketchbook is the ideal place to keep all your ideas, from words, to colour experiments, to stitches. As you document your thoughts you will also develop your own working method. If you look back over your notes they may inspire new mixed-media artworks.

I use my sketchbook as a starting point as it is where I begin to think about the concepts which will be the basis of a piece of art. I collect magazine cuttings, interesting fabrics and papers, and found objects. It is surprising how quickly I developed an eye for anything that might be useful as part of an artwork, or as inspiration for one.

Your sketchbook is the ideal place to explore ideas and techniques as you will not be concerned about what the end result will be. This is your chance to use your imagination; each page will soon vary in style. Documenting your thought processes is vital, whether through quick sketches or brainstorming sessions. I often write lists of materials or words that go on to trigger useful ideas when I begin to experiment with materials. I may add research from the Internet, or photocopies from books, too.

DRAWING

Drawing is a very important technique. Many of the mixed-media designs in this book began with a line drawing, which is then interpreted in stitch or in print. If you are not confident with a pen or pencil, find an image that inspires you and trace it.

Shape, colour, texture and scale should also be explored as part of the initial design process.

Shape

Looking at shape is a great starting point for a arranging a composition. If you are a beginner, you can explore how particular shapes create boundaries, and if so, whether these lines will determine a different colour or texture. Stencilling is a great way to add shapes onto a surface, maybe to symbolise an object or meaning in your work. For example, you may wish to use rectangles to represent the human form in a simplistic way.

Texture

Texture swatches are important when you are brainstorming initial concepts. You may find it useful to place colour and texture swatches alongside drawings in your sketchbook to help visualise how they would work as a final piece.

Scale

The impact and detail of a piece can simply be down to the size of your 'canvas'. Think about how heavy your lines will be in relation to the details in your composition and how well it relates to your concept. For example hand stitch could be overwhelmed in a very large work, unless you're trying to achieve very delicate detail.

TIP ⌇ My work is based on my love for beautiful fabrics and is heavily influenced by fashion and literature. However, you may take your inspiration from nature or an important event in your life, and your concept can be as simple – or as complex – as you like.

TIP ❯ Rough sketches are the best way to develop a composition. Use them to experiment with structure, layers and the juxtaposition of materials to create exciting visual effects.

TIP ❯ Use images torn from newspapers or photocopies of original material when experimenting with composition as this allows you to make mistakes inexpensively.

COMPOSITION

The projects in this book show the importance of composition.
The way in which I compose my artworks is inspired by the work of
photographer and designer Faye Heller. She splits an image into
sections and juxtaposes these with sections of other photographs
to create new images, such as in the work below, called *Trim Close*
(see www.fayeheller.com to find out more). However, there are
many other ways to make composition interesting.

Many of the projects in this book feature a structured composition of vertical strips and squares. I choose to work with different sized rectangles and squares, applying images and textures in various ways. The process of layering and juxtaposing creates exciting visual effects. You might want to introduce different shapes such as circles, which combine successfully with linear shapes.

COLOUR

The colours you want to use for a mixed-media artwork may be one of the first things you consider. The choice may be obvious – if your concept is 'nature' for example, you might choose greens and nude, natural colours. Similarly, some of my projects were inspired by the book *The Handmaid's Tale* (1985) by Margaret Atwood. The many references to blood, torture and love within the narrative meant it was unavoidable that the colour red was used in the final illustrations.

Beginners may wish to pick a tonal palette and add vibrant block colours later. An inexpensive way to experiment with colour is to collect paint sample cards, available from DIY stores, and place them side-by-side. This is an easy way to move colours around to see how they look against each other. The next step is to start mixing paint colours together.

EXPERIMENTATION

Exploring your ideas before you begin your final piece will introduce you to basic techniques and help to develop your own unique style. Experimentation is vital, especially when exploring mixed-media design, as what at first appears to be a mistake may become a new way of working with a beautiful finish.

I often make a series of a particular design using inexpensive materials. One quick and easy way I do this is to photocopy my first experiment several times. These copies can then be manipulated and explored by printing or painting onto them, and even stitching through parts of them for a sense of the final look. Often photocopies bring out their own interesting finishes that can also contribute to a final piece.

Once you are ready to start making the final piece, go back through your sketchbook to identify the most effective compositions, colour and techniques. Remember your tests may have introduced new design problems that you will have to work around or dismiss, but do not forget these completely as they may come in handy for another project.

TIP ꞉ Blocks of paint are inexpensive and perfect to use when trying out colour palettes for a new composition.

PROJECTS

5

Angel: stain,
print, sew

This project uses everyday household materials to create an interesting background for mono printing and stitching. You can adapt the colours, but this project creates a delicate effect that works best when made with a subtle palette, reserving vibrant colours for the stitched outline. This project can be created with very little equipment.

MATERIALS

- Baking paper
- Coffee
- Tissue or cotton wool
- Mono print ink
- Ink roller
- Cuttings from magazines, photos, or other images that inspire you
- Pencil
- Sewing machine
- Thread

INSPIRATION

Think about what atmosphere the colours you choose will create. I have used a colour palette that creates a very calm and peaceful mood. The printed image of an angel seemed a powerful yet restrained one to overlay on top of the subtle background. Chose an image that you connect with; you may want to look through your research materials, in magazines or at picture postcards for inspiration. This type of mono print looks great at any size and can be used as artwork to decorate wall.

1 Cut a sheet of non-stick baking paper to the desired size and shape of your background. Make it slightly larger than the finished artwork so that you can trim it to give a neat edge later.

TIP ❯ Think about the composition of your artwork. You may prefer to leave blank area to display the effect of the baked tracing paper.

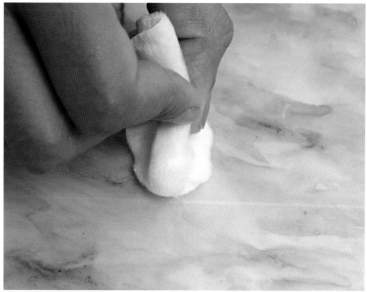

2 Prepare some instant coffee and, using tissue or cotton wool, apply liberally to the paper. Leave to dry. Repeat the process, making sure you cover the surface completely. This creates a crinkled and uneven finish.

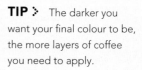

TIP ❯ The darker you want your final colour to be, the more layers of coffee you need to apply.

3 Turn on the oven at a low heat (gas mark 5). Place the coffee-stained paper on to the oven shelf and leave to bake, being careful it does not burn. The longer you heat the paper, the darker the finish. Leaving the paper in for 5 minutes will create a lighter effect and leaving it in for 10–15 minutes will create a darker and more crinkled finish. You will need to use a bit of trial and error as all ovens vary!

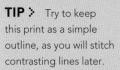

TIP ⸱› Try to keep this print as a simple outline, as you will stitch contrasting lines later.

4 Create a mono print onto your background using the method explained in the Techniques section (see p.32).

5 Leave the surface to dry
and then gently use a pencil
to sketch onto the print where
you would like to add stitching.
The stitches can add detail or
be part of the main design.

6 Add further details using
pieces of fabric or handmade
paper. These can be glued, or
stitched to create further depth
to your image. Think carefully
about the composition – do
not to add anything too

overpowering: small, thin strips
or small circles and squares of
material work well to create
subtle details.

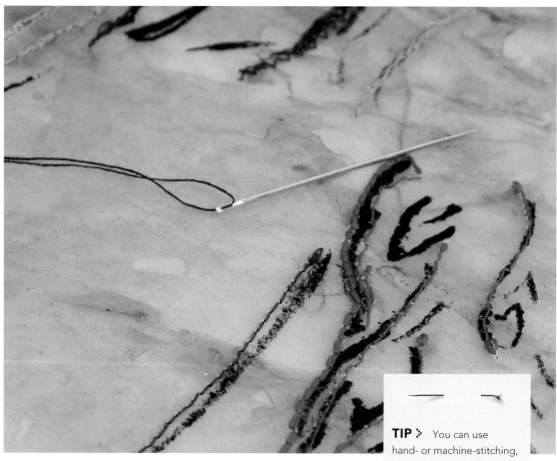

TIP ➤ You can use
hand- or machine-stitching,
using different stitches
and machine feet and
different thread colours.
(See Technique chapter,
pp.27–31). You may wish to
create controlled stitches
or a much more free and
creative line.

Hansel & Gretel:
tear, shape, write

This project shows you how to incorporate simple materials such as paper into your artwork. Choose your own images and subjects to design your own images. Experiment with beads and hand-stitching to add details. This project can be created with very little technique, but imagination and creativity are key. A beginner can complete this project with ease.

INSPIRATION

For this project think about vibrant, simple images on which to base your piece. I have decided to use children's storybook characters Hansel and Gretel as a starting point here. Block colours in bold shapes cut from different papers and fabrics are perfect for creating playful collages. They can easily be layered and then embellished with beads and stitching.

MATERIALS

- Canvas for the background
- Tracing paper
- Selection of coloured card and paper
- Fabrics
- Fabric glue
- Beads and sequins
- Needle and embroidery thread
- Fine-liner pen
- Hole punch
- Scissors

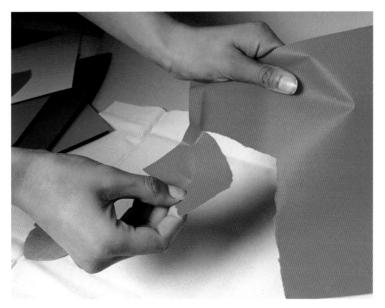

1 Cut out the background material. When choosing the material think about the base colour, and bear in mind that a thin material, such as canvas or handmade paper, often works best for backgrounds, as it will be easier to stitch through when more layers have been added.

2 Tear out the collage shapes for your image. Coloured card, magazines and handmade paper all work well together and create interesting effects.

TIP You may want to trace around an image to use as a template before you begin tearing out the separate pieces to create your final image.

3 Create shading to add depth to your image using several different colours of paper, shaped with careful tearing.

TIP Try using a hole punch to create small circles.

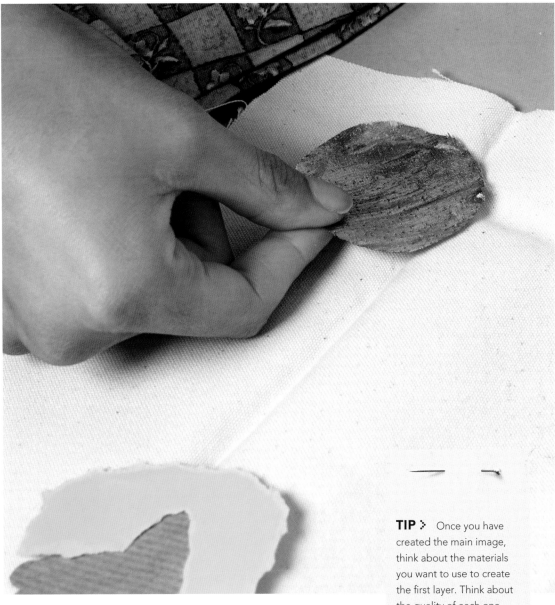

4 Use fabric glue to attach the collage to your background and leave it to dry.

TIP ❯ Once you have created the main image, think about the materials you want to use to create the first layer. Think about the quality of each one and how it will represent part of the scene you are creating. For example, silks create a luxurious effect, while hessian gives a vintage, rustic feel.

5 Add details taken from printed fabrics or magazine pages. Try pieces of floral fabric, or pictures of accessories such as ribbons from fashion magazines.

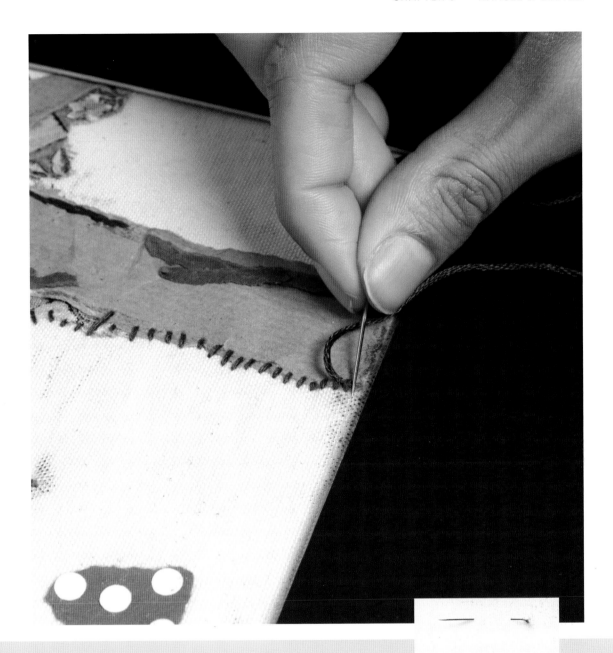

6 Once the glue has dried, embroider details to highlight areas of your image.

TIP > In simple designs such as this, hand stitching contrasts well with the bold shapes in the collage. Try a variety of hand stitches – they do not have to be perfect.

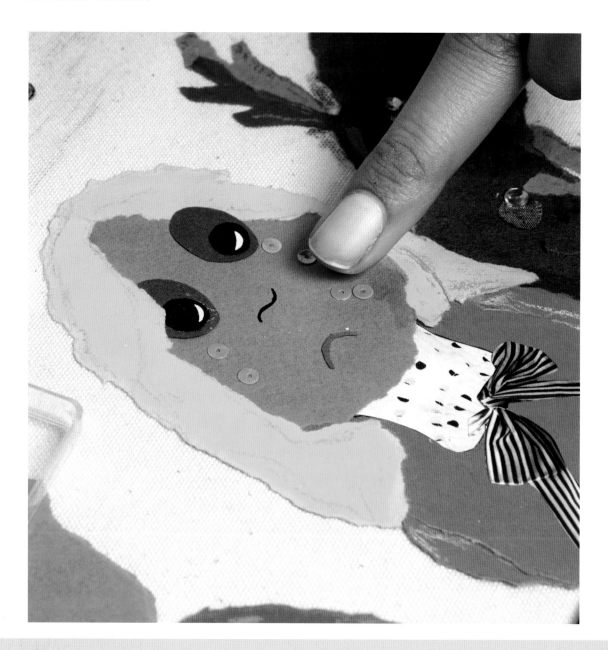

7 Beads and sequins add quirky details and finishing touches.

That night, when the moonlight shone through the trees, the pebbles Hansel had dropped gleamed like silver coins. The children followed the trail all the way back to their parents' cottage.

8 If you are adding text to your image, use a fine-liner pen, or try stitching the words.

When Hansel and Gretel awoke, dusk was falling and there was no sign of their parents. 'We will never find our way home alone,' sobbed Gretel. 'Just wait,' said Hansel.

That night, when the moonlight shone through the trees, the pebbles Hansel had dropped gleamed like silver coins. The children followed the trail all the way back to their parents' cottage.

... room with two cosy beds they were fast asleep.

1984: rip, draw, distress

This project explores layering by contrasting different weights of paper. Experiment with print, pencils and crayons to create interesting images. This project can be adapted for your own colour scheme and inspiration.

INSPIRATION

Think about something you love and how you'd like to represent it in the image you create. The book *1984* by George Orwell (1949) inspired this illustration. However, the concept for the project can be easily adapted. Start with a clear, simple drawing. Alternatively, arrange a collection of found objects into a still life and take a photograph, print it from a computer, and transfer the oulines in the picture to your background using the mono print technique (see p.32).

MATERIALS

- Cardboard
- Matches
- Ink, pencils, wax crayons
- Tracing paper
- Mono print ink
- Ink roller
- Watercolour and/or acrylic paints and a paintbrush
- Glue
- Embroidery thread
- Needle
- Scraps of fabric
- Slightly sharp object such as a craft knife or needle

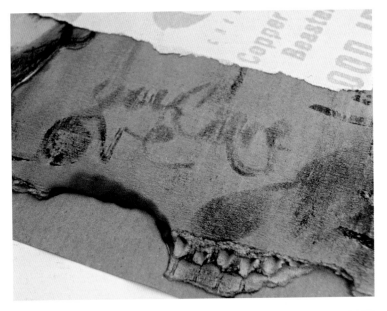

1 Take some old cardboard and carefully tear out a rough square. Carefully burn around the edges to achieve a natural yet rough edge.

TIP ❯ Be careful when burning the edges. Use safety matches and light them in an open space – preferably over the sink so that water is accessible to extinguish the flame if necessary. You may need to experiment to get the edge you require.

2 Prepare your first layer, thinking carefully about your colour palette. Try using darker colours, and work freely to create interesting effects and unusual shades. You may prefer to use ink or wax crayons to achieve a less polished, rougher finish.

TIP ❯ Mixing paints directly on to the cardboard will result in a subtle yet textured finish.

TIP ❯ Your sketchbook is important here. Think about different compositions. This first layer should contain plenty of visual interest yet not overpower the finished artwork.

3 Prepare the next layer while the background paint and layers dry. Take a different weight of paper – tracing paper or another transparent paper works well – and mono print, draw or paint an image onto it.

4 Once this image is dry, scratch into parts of it using a sharp object such as a blunt blade. This will give the surface a worn look and can be used if you want to scratch away some of the mono print to break up the design.

TIP ⸖ When scratching the surface do not use anything too sharp as it may tear the paper.

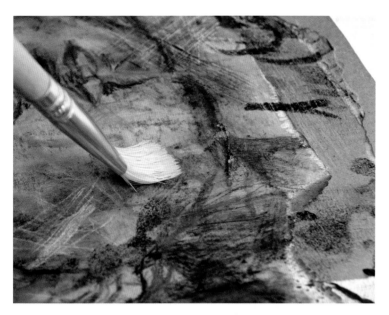

5 Next apply colour using paints and crayons. Work freely on top of the image to create interesting finishes. You may choose to distort your original image completely.

6 Leave to dry, then repeat this process until you have created an interesting and textured finish.

TIP Take care when combining colours. Always stick to your colour palette and use a maximum of four colours. Leave some areas un-worked to break up the composition – while you don't want the finished composition to appear flat, be careful not to over manipulate it.

7 Once your background is dry add layers and detail using simple shapes. This works well with text created on a computer and printed on to vibrant paper.

8 Carefully glue each layer of your composition together.

TIP ❯ You may also want to repeat Step 4 and scratch out parts of the lettering.

9 Apply stencilling to the surface. The simplest method is to cut out the shape you wish to add from a piece of scrap paper to create a stencil. Position the stencil and hold firmly in place with one hand. Dip the tip of a paintbrush into the paint and apply. If you're confident you could try building up the pattern by overlaying stencilled shapes.

TIP ❯ Think how you might use other materials to highlight parts of your composition. Try using pieces of canvas to contrast with the darker areas.

10 Add further details with hand stitching. Use two strands of embroidery thread for a chunky stitch. You can keep your stitching simple, or explore different stitches – the amount of detail and types of stitch are up to you.

You could work freely or create neat, controlled stitching around certain areas of your image.

TIP ⫶ The most common stencil brushes have flat and domed bristles. Be careful – too much paint on the brush causes blotchy designs.

Try stippling the paint, by tapping or dabbing the brush against the stencil. This tends to produce more even tones and less depth; or swirling, using circular brush motions against the stencil.

Varying the amount of pressure or paint you apply with your brush will create different effects. Shading can add depth and interest to your stencilled designs. Applying the paint with different materials such as cotton wool or a sponge will also give you a different finish. Again, change the amount of paint and pressure to vary the result.

11 Add finishing touches such as beads and metal studs attached with glue. This adds an almost precious feeling to the design. Use them as part of your design, to highlight an area, or to add line and shape.

8 _____ *The Handmaid's Tale:*
layer, burn, unpick

This project uses soft textile shapes and machine stitching and a variety of subtle colours to create a natural-looking background. This project will suit those with experience in machine stitching.

INSPIRATION

This piece highlights the qualities of different fabrics and shows how they can be combined to create a dramatic finish. It was inspired by a character from the book *The Handmaid's Tale* by Margaret Atwood (1985) but you could look for inspiration in nature, or drawings from your sketchbook. To increase the drama, be sure to choose a significant shape for your outline – I chose the silhouette of a woman in a handmaid's uniform. This shape needs to recognisable as it will transition from strong colours and solid line, to a distressed, almost ghostly outline. The shape should also be easy to manipulate as each variation uses a different technique. The impression of the outline being interrupted or unravelling as you read it from left to right will intrigue the viewer, but you could equally start with the outline frayed and indistinct at the left and progress to a bolder shape onon the right.

TIP ❯ I worked out the composition for this piece in my sketchbook first. From my experiments I discovered I liked a vertical background with empty space above the silhouettes. Use your sketchbook to help you plan your composition.

MATERIALS

- A selection of card and paper (try wrapping paper or wallpaper)
- A selection of fabrics (chiffon, silk and net work well)
- Scissors
- Pins
- Tracing or non-stick baking paper
- Coffee
- Safety matches
- Paint and paintbrush
- Sewing machine and thread
- Thread

1 Collect a variety of different fabrics and papers and put together a selection that complement each other.

TIP ⸙ Thinking about the layers you will add later will help you to choose a colour palette for the background and decide how much detail to include.

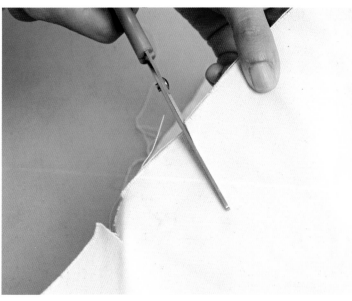

2 Cut the background material – stiff fabric or card are good – to your desired size and shape. Think about how you might display this work when it is complete: if you plan to put it in a picture frame you could measure it to fit.

3 Build up the first layer with long strips of contrasting texture. Use coffee to stain a piece of non-stick baking paper (see 'Angel' project, pp.46–7). Wetting and drying the paper in the oven creates a wrinkled surface bringing texture to the first layer. It also bulks up the layer beneath or on top of it. Tear neatly along a straight edge to create a strip and glue it onto your background.

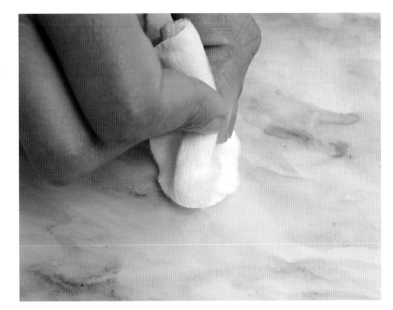

4 Take some textured paper such as tissue paper or brown paper and tear it in to strips; add texture by creasing some or all of these. Carefully glue to your background. The tissue paper can be applied flat and then gently shaped and manipulated while still wet to add texture. Also consider printing text onto some paper, or using patterned wallpaper or wrapping paper, then layering tissue paper over the top.

TIP ❯ Tea, watercolour paints and dyes are great methods you can use to colour tracing paper if you are not using baking paper.

TIP ❯ Tissue paper does not need to be neatly applied. As it is such a thin paper try layering different colours on top of one another.

5 Take a strip of fabric and carefully burn through random parts using a match. This works well with a variety of fabrics but ensure your fabric is not flammable before you start, so you can control the burning. Do this over the sink so that you have a supply of water near by to put out the flame if necessary. Glue this strip alongside your layered strips of paper prepared in the previous steps. The first layer is now complete.

TIP ⌖ If necessary, add torn pieces of plain papers or fabrics to disguise frayed edges and obvious, unwanted joins.

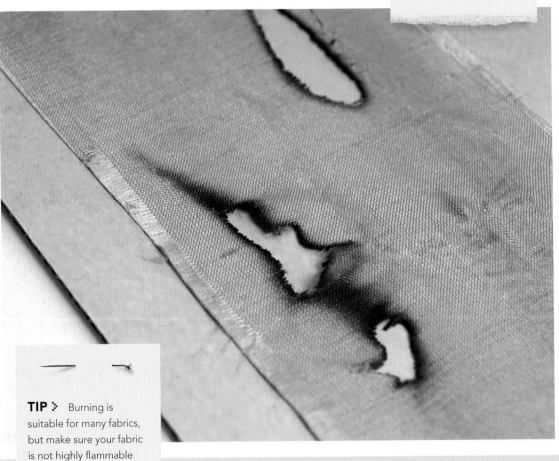

TIP ⌖ Burning is suitable for many fabrics, but make sure your fabric is not highly flammable first! If in doubt, do not experiment. You may find it easier to burn a large piece of fabric and then choose a section that fits your composition.

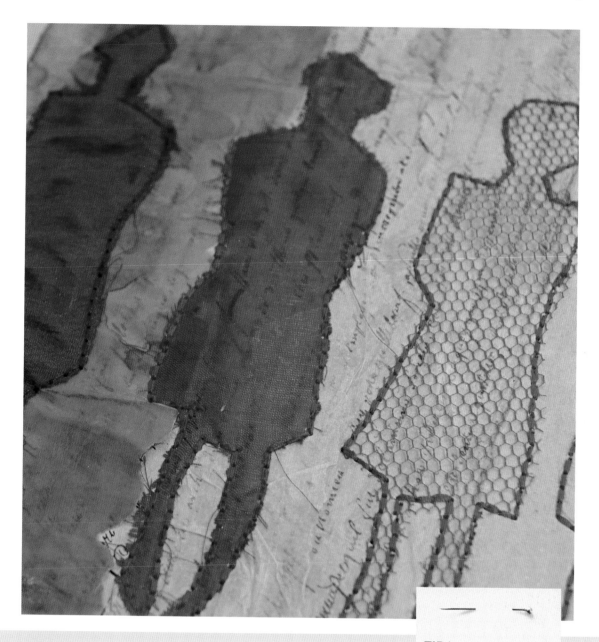

6 Assemble a variety
of fabrics with different
thicknesses and colours. In this
example, red silk, chiffon and
net have been used.

TIP ⊱ Using a range of
fabrics and colours prevents
the picture becoming
flat. Note that patterned
fabrics may overpower the
illustration so experiment
with layering and position
in your sketchbook first.

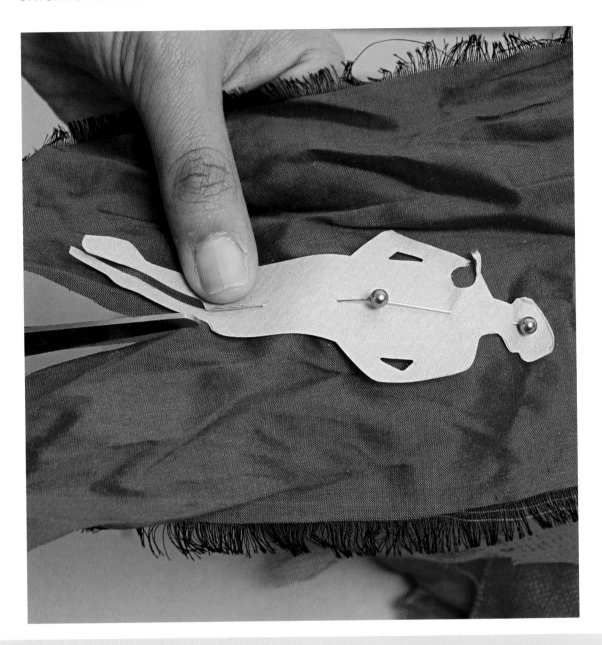

7 Create a paper template of your selected shape and use as a pattern to cut from your chosen fabrics. You may prefer to draw on to the fabric using a fabric chalk rather than pinning the pattern to the fabric if the outline is fiddly.

A paper template allows you to experiment with the composition.

8 Sew around the edges of the shapes using a machine straight stitch, or similar simple stitch. Using small, neat stitches will contrast with the textured and random background.

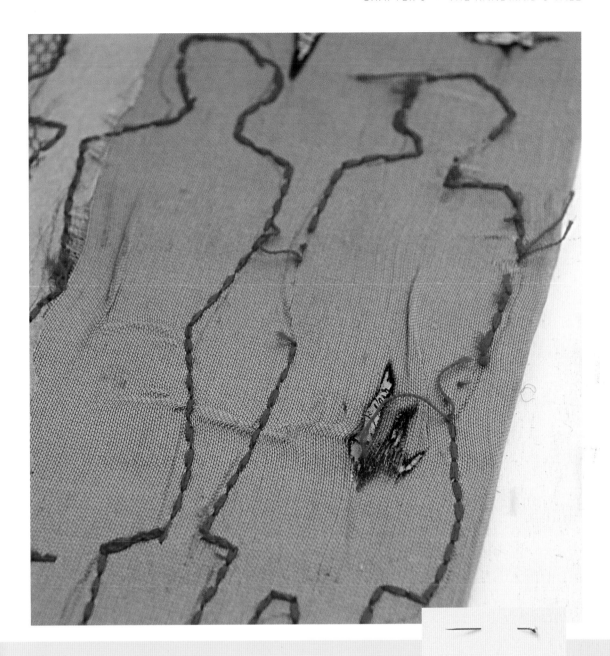

9 Draw around the template in chalk or pencil onto the surface prepared in Steps 3–5. Using the same stitch as in Step 8, follow your chalk or pencil guidelines to stitch in two outlines of your shape.

VARIATION

Beginners may want to use a hand running stitch for Steps 8 and 9. Or you can mix machine- and hand-stitching for an interesting finish.

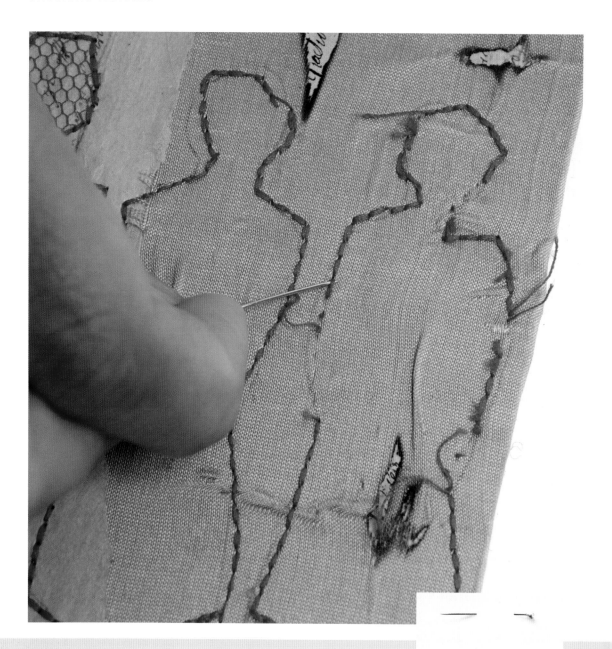

10 Unpick some of the stitching of one of the figures to create the effect of the outline unravelling.

11 Cut off any loose threads.

12 Glue the fabric silhouettes prepared in Steps 7 and 8 alongside the stitched outline. You can position them in any order, but I have placed the silhouettes so that they get bolder from left to right.

TIP ❯ You may want to add further detail to the area of background you have outlined. Alternatively you may want to keep this section simple and bold.

Freedom:
laminate, stencil, stitch

This project shows you how to incorporate simple stencilling and stitching techniques to create a design. Choose your own colours, images and fabrics to make your own variation: there are plenty of possibilities. This project can be created with very little equipment.

INSPIRATION

To get your creativity flowing, think about using your interests, hobbies or a subject you are passionate about as the focus of this piece. In my illustration I decided to think about how fashion represents the feminine form. I kept this picture small (15 x 10cm/6 x 4in.) so it could be reproduced on items such a cards and gift tags. It was created as four separate pieces but came together as one piece when each section was glued on to a piece of cardboard at the end. The number of sections you choose to make is up to you, although only four sections are described in the project that follows.

MATERIALS

- Cardboard
- Acrylic paint
- Fabric scraps (silk is good)
- Sewing machine
- Thread
- Tracing paper
- Glue
- Laminate sheets
- Photocopier
- Scissors
- Mono print ink and roller
- Magazine cuttings

1 Prepare each section of your work. Use your sketchbook to decide how each section will look and what techniques you'd like to try. Think about the overall composition and how the sections will work together.

Remember you do not want to overpower any one part of the design with heavy detail and textures.

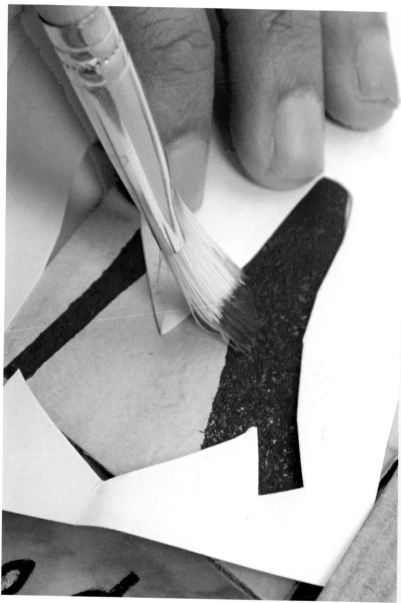

2 Create your first section. This will be a stencil print onto a piece of cardboard.

Cut out your desired shape from a piece of paper and place on top of the background, holding it flat with your fingers. Apply the paint, carefully remove the stencil and leave to dry.

TIP ❯ Think carefully about the materials and colours you use – stencilling always looks more effective when kept simple. Bear in mind the texture and colour – a heavily textured background will detract from the simplicity of your stencil. Handmade paper and pieces of coloured card in matching shades are more suitable. Also consider the colours and the different ways you can apply the paint. You may wish to try different-sized brushes (depending on the size of your work, household brushes are a great way to create texture), rollers, spray paint, and other materials such as cardboard, cotton wool, and even your fingers!

3 For your second section, create a small scrap of lettering. Find a typeface you like in a magazine, or print out some sample fonts from a computer. Carefully cut out the letters using a Stanley knife to create a stencil. Stencil the letters onto onto tracing paper for a semi-translucent effect. You could try staining the tracing paper with tea first.

4 Next, create a detailed and intricate section for your image to contrast with the flatter, stencilled sections.

Create a simple stitch 'drawing' on a scrap of fabric. Try double stitching using the sewing machine to create a simple but bold outline. Remember that the stitches will be a very prominent part of the design, so ensure your lines are neat and simple for the most effective finish.

I have stitched around a red piece of fabric for a skirt, and added legs and high heels in double stitching.

TIP > If you don't want to stencil your text you can mono print the letters onto your background. (See Techniques chapter, p.32.)

TIP > You could also use fabric or paint to create blocks of colour, or to mask part of your image.

5 The fourth section is another contrast because it is made from a shiny laminate sheet that has been photocopied onto. The photocopy will appear much more intense than it would on copier paper. Most stationery shops stock laminate and it is compatible with most photocopiers. Photocopy a close-up of a striking image onto a sheet of laminate. Enhance it with stitch or paint.

TIP > The amount of detail and types of stitching on your laminate are up to you. You may choose to stitch freely over the image, or to follow an outline. Think about ways to introduce colour – a bold, vibrant shade of thread always looks effective over the black and transparent image created by the laminate photocopy.

6 Once you have created all your sections, move them around to see which arrangement you like best. You may want to try having some sections overlap. Cut a piece of cardboard to the right size for your composition and then glue the sections down. The laminate can be stitched onto your background, or simply glued on at the corners.

10

Catwalk: colour,
collage embellish

This project combines layers of paint and printing with fabrics. You can adapt it by thinking about where it will be displayed and choosing your colours and materials accordingly.

INSPIRATION

This is a project is a great place to start exploring colour combinations, fabric compositions and simple machine stitching. It was influenced by fashion, and in particular the work of Vivienne Westwood. I have used some of the ways in which she creates detail – for example, torn fabrics, asymmetric compositions, safety pin detailing and stitching – and sourced materials similar to those she uses in her designs. You may want to include objects such as safety pins to give an edge to your final piece.

MATERIALS

- Canvas
- Paints
- A selection of fabrics and paper
- Craft/garden wire
- Safety pins
- Sewing machine
- Thread
- Embellishments such as beads, studs or gems
- Mono print ink and roller
- Magazine cuttings
- Hole punch
- Scissors

1 Cut a piece of canvas to the desired size, allowing a 5cm (2in) border which can be pulled tight around a wooden frame and stapled into place once the artwork is complete.

2 Prepare the background by gluing a range of different textures, such as handmade paper, denim scraps and old photographs, to the canvas. This will give the work a gorgeous tactile effect.

TIP A fragmented background consisting of different colours, shapes and textures will be dynamic and have strong visual appeal.

3 Next, add a layer of paint. Think about your colour palette and how the paint will be applied before you start. The painted layer should avoid overpowering the rest of the design. Subtle colour palettes such as neutrals are easy to work with, but bold colours have the advantage of not disappearing if you choose to layer detail on top of them at a later stage. Try using different types of brush, and to get a unique range of colour you could mix the paints directly on the canvas, rather than before applying them. To create depth, allow the first layer of paint to dry before adding a second.

TIP ⟩ Experiment with colour in your sketchbook (see pp.22–5 and p.41). Subdued colours look good juxtaposed with darker shades. More vibrant shades can be used to add instant design features.

4 When the paint is dry, apply a mono print to to the surface. There are many ways to do this, but the method I use to create a rough image is explained in the Techniques section (see p.32). Both text and images can be created using this method.

5 Once your printed layer is dry, build up the surface further by attaching simple shapes to break up the composition even more. Try cutting circles and squares from different fabrics such as a pair of old denim jeans or a tartan skirt.

TIP ⯈ Try creating an outline for your mono print by tracing an outline from a section of a photograph or a magazine page. Lay your image over a scrap of paper covered with ink, and using a pencil or pen, carefully follow the parts of the image that you want to transfer. Pressing harder in some places, and with different tools, creates additional effects.

TIP ⯈ This particular piece was inspired by fashion. I decided to take my own pictures of models in particular poses and then used these as these an outline for my prints. Old photographs are also a great way to create personal pieces of art.

6 Add detail with machine stitching. Work freely over your composition with a variety of stitches to create highlights, outlines and shadows.

TIP ⟩ Experiment with a standard presser foot and zigzag stitch, working backwards and forwards to create an interesting line, like the red line in this picture (right). Alternatively, using a darning foot will allow you to embroider in any direction. See the manual of your machine for instructions for using a darning foot.

7 If you're feeling adventurous you could try cutting a hole in the canvas. This can be left unfilled, or you could add safety pins or place a tactile fabric such as silk or net behind the hole. This can easily be secured using fabric glue around the edges.

8 Add finishing touches such as safety pins, and use coloured papers to create dashed of vibrant colour.

TIP ❯ For even more detail, tear the paper, or use a hole punch.

91

9 Think about other materials you can use to highlight parts of your composition. Try pushing wire through the canvas to add depth and further enhance its visual appeal.

These three pieces were all made using the techniques described in this project. They were influenced by the world of fashion – models on the catwalk, text from magazines, and detailing from couture garments such as buttons and fastenings.

Dark hues were juxtaposed with neutral ones, offset by tartan prints and bright details.

11

Statement layers:
combine, cut, arrange

This project explores the layering of a variety of materials and experiments with different surfaces to create some of the most interesting surface effects. It is constructed of individually composed squares and rectangles put together at the end in these long wall hangings. Each square or rectangular panel was thought about separately as a collage of mixed materials embellished with textile techniques and paint. Add variety to your wall hanging by choosing your own colours and textures, and do not be afraid to try out new techniques, or to work each layer more than once.

MATERIALS

- A selection of fabrics
- A selection of papers
- Cuttings and photographs that have inspired you
- Spray paint
- Laminate
- Mono print ink
- Ink roller
- Dylon Image Maker (available from most craft shops)
- Scissors
- Sewing machine
- Thread
- Ribbon

INSPIRATION

This project is a great way to explore all your favourite techniques. Here, again, I was influenced by fashion, culture and many of the people around me: your friends, colleagues, and even favourite celebrities are a great source on inspiration. You may want to record a special event like a birthday or holiday. The scale of this hanging will alter the composition, so think about the shapes and number of panels you would like to use.

1 Work out a basic composition in your sketchbook. You may wish to use inexpensive materials such as magazine pages or photocopies to prepare your design. (See Developing your Ideas, pp.36–41). The piece can be as simple as three squares, but more experienced artists may wish to use many more panels.

2 The base layer of many of the panels is a photocopy of a collage made on acetate. Acetate is a great material to use because it gives good results for photocopies but has more depth and creates more atmosphere than paper. It can also be worked over successfully with further techniques. Tracing paper can also be used. Prepare the material which will be the main part of your composition. Here acetate has been used as it is easy to manipulate layered effectively. Tearing up magazine pages and layering different fabrics together and then photocopying them can create interesting finishes.

TIP ❯ It is important to remember that this part of your composition should not be too textured or have too much pattern as it is only the first layer.

3 Create a collage from pieces of paper or fabrics. I used magazine cuttings. Work out the arrangement then carefully transfer it face down to the bed of the photocopier. Photocopy onto acetate, then check you are happy with the results before removing the collage from the photocopier. Repeat using different materials until you have several small photocopied compositions.

TIP You may want to photocopy original pieces of your artwork to use in this design. Some of the other projects in this book would be perfect for this.

4 Assemble the other papers, fabrics, paints, threads and so on you want to use in your remaining panels. You can either try out the techniques in your sketchbook, or work directly on to your composition. Remember here that mistakes often result in some of the most exciting finishes. For each panel you want to make cut a square or rectangle of paper, card or fabric to a little larger than you want for your panel, so that you can attach it to other parts of your design. Steps 5–8 describe different ways to design the panels using a range of techniques.

5 Make a mono print. There are many ways to do this, but the method I use to create a rough image is explained in the Techniques section (see p.32).

TIP You may want to manipulate some of the areas while the ink is still wet. You can do this by adding additional ink on top, or scratching onto the surface with a blunt blade or the tip of an old paintbrush. Or try printing onto a magazine page or photograph.

6 Create a fabric print using a transfer product like Dylon Image Maker. This allows you to tranfer a photocopy or laser print to a fabric surface. Instructions are included with the product and it's quick to do but will need to be left to dry overnight.

TIP Using Image Maker on an image printed in a magazine results in a lighter, more distressed look, than if you use an image printed from a computer.

7 Stencil onto card or plain or patterned wallpaper (see p.35).

8 Glue cuttings from magazines, old photographs and scraps of wrapping paper to a base of fabric or card. As the materials are relatively inexpensive you can afford to play around with them.

TIP ⊁ Scratching into photographs, or using ink and paint on top of the paper, is a simple way to create interesting finishes.

9 Continue experimenting and creating small pieces of artwork until you have enough panels to construct your composition.

TIP ❯ Be sure to think about the different textures and effects you want. Take care that one part of your composition does not become overly detailed. Try out different arrangements to see what works best.

10 You can glue or stitch your composition together, bearing in mind that any stitching will add to the final finish.

11 Add detail to your composition by:

Cutting shapes into parts of it and layering materials behind the cutouts to add colour and texture.

Using a stencil to spray-paint simple shapes such as circles over parts of your artwork.

Stitching, by hand or machine, around some areas. Zigzag stitch is very effective here.

12 If you want to, choose a background material for your wall hanging and sew it on. I have used a subtle shade of pink chiffon crêpe to complement some of the colours in the design. Any lightweight fabric in a pale shade would do – try cottons, crêpe or even silk if you want to give your hanging a luxury feel. Finally, attach ribbons at the top so you can hang this on the wall.

12

Portrait: appliqué,
paint, pattern

Project by Alexandra Hutch · *rabbithutchdesigns.co.uk*

INSPIRATION

First decide on the subject matter for your artwork. I have chosen a portrait, but something more abstract based on plants or animals works well too.

MATERIALS

- Variety of fabrics
- Sewing machine
- Iron
- Thread
- Bondaweb
- Tracing paper
- Embroidery thread (optional)
- Lace or other trimmings (optional)
- Fabric paint (optional)

1 Start creating a design on paper. Look in magazines and books for inspiration; you could copy or trace an image you like or draw your own. Decide on the composition, thinking about the shape, scale and layout of your piece. You may want to crop your design and focus on one section only: a paper viewfinder will help you with this.

2 When creating your design, think about the areas where you will draw lines using stitches, where you will create texture by building up stitches, which areas you will paint, and the areas where you'll leave the fabric exposed.

Ideally there will be a balance so that one technique does not overpower your piece.

TIP ✣ Once you are happy with your design, it's a good idea to make a photocopy to use as a template. You can also use the photocopier to adjust the scale – especially useful for enlarging it.

3 Choose the materials you'd like to use by selecting fabrics and threads in colours and patterns that will complement your design.

4 Now it's time to think about the process of creating your piece. Decide on how you will break up your design into separate shapes of fabric and whether you will need to layer them up.

Decide which of the following techniques you will use. The order in which you use them depends on your design. Bear in mind that if you're using fabric paint, you'll need to let it dry before sewing onto it.

5 Appliqué shapes onto the background using Bondaweb. Transfer each separate shape from your design onto the Bondaweb using a pencil and tracing paper. Iron the Bondaweb onto the fabric you have chosen for the shapes. Cut out the shapes, following the traced outline, peel the backing off the Bondaweb and place it onto your background fabric. Iron to secure it in place.

6 Use fabric paint to add more shapes. Mix the shades you require, keeping the paint watery to start with so that you can build up colour.

TIP ⟩ Always test the paint on a scrap of the fabric first to see what the affect will be.

7 Add detail and texture with stitching. To sew lines, first draw them onto the fabric using fabric chalk to act as a guide. Then sew along each line, either by free embroidery on the sewing machine, or by hand.

Add stitched texture using free embroidery on the sewing machine, but try experimenting on another piece of fabric beforehand.

TIP ⸴ You will be able to gain different effects by using straight stitch or zigzag, and by varying how quickly you move the fabric on the machine. The slower you move the fabric, the more thickly texture will build up. Try building up colour by stitching different coloured threads on top of each other. You can also incorporate wool or embroidery thread by holding it in place and stitching over it to secure it, as has been done here for the hair.

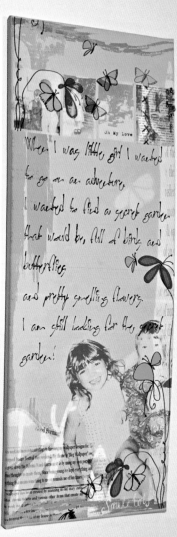

Project by Sammy-Jane Kenney · *sammyjanekenny.blogspot.com*

This project shows you how to use simple everyday materials to create your own personalized wall art. This project can be created with very little equipment and could be used to record a special event, experience or memory.

INSPIRATION

Pieces of art can be very personal, both to you and the subject. Think about different items or belongings that represent you as a person. These can be anything from bus tickets to photographs, diary cuttings and old letters.

TIP ⋗ Be creative when you are collecting items to use in your work. Think about light objects that hold memories about a time, person or place, for example hair clips, unwanted jigsaw puzzle pieces or playing cards, birthday cards, clothing labels, packaging, bottle tops, badges, shells, pressed flowers etc.

MATERIALS

- A variety of papers
- Collection of personal items (see tip box)
- Glue
- Paint
- Roller brush
- Black fine-liner pen
- Large and small needles
- Coloured wool
- Beads
- Cotton

1 Prepare the background material for your composition. You may wish to cut or tear the background to create an interesting finish.

TIP ❯ Remember to think about the techniques you will use and the weight of your objects before deciding on a background material. For example, cardboard would work well for heavier objects, while handmade paper would be perfect for a delicate composition.

2 Add colour to your background by using a roller brush apply a thin, uneven layer of paint.

TIP ❯ If you want to experiment with colour combinations, remember to let each layer dry first. You may also want to try using the darkest shade first; this will create defined layers.

Photographs on this page and opposite ©: Sammy-Jane Kenny

3 Using your collected items, create a collage on the painted background. Try to create a theme throughout the piece to tell a story, e.g. photographs with diary cuttings, clothes tags with bits of old fabric and so on.

TIP ❯ Play around with combinations, you may wish to sketch a few ideas in your sketchbook. It is important to remember not to overpower one part of the image.

4 Once you are happy with your composition use PVA glue to stick the items down.

5 Stand back and take a look at your piece. If you think there is an area of empty space use a black fine liner pen to fill that space with some words. Choose an appropriate writing style and write anything from poems you like, lyrics, horoscropes etc.

TIP › If you find it hard to place items, hold them all in your hands, stand over the background and drop them. This will give a great collage feel and – if you think it looks a bit bare – you can work into it further later on.

TIP › If you do not feel confident with free-hand writing, use a computer to print off single letters and glue them down to create the words you want to say. It helps to plan this in your sketchbook.

6 Using a large needle and coloured wool, sew around a few of the items that have been glued down. A simple running stitch will look very effective and will give a nice three-dimensional, layered effect.

TIP ⟩ If you are confident with a sewing machine, you may wish to try sewing words into the photographs/letters. Think about the different colours and wool thickness.

7 Using a small needle and cotton, apply to beads to add a finishing touch to your wall piece. You could even experiment by arranging them in patterns or as letters.

Photographs on this page and opposite ©: Sammy-Jane Kenny

TIP ⟩ Adding small studs or even safety pins adds quirky detail.

GALLERY

COS AHMET

My compositions are assembled from and inspired by my diverse personal archive of postcards, found imagery, newsprint/magazine cuttings and fabric remnants, amongst other things. I find that a combination of chance and pure experimentation can sometimes conjure up unexpected results, and that is when the magic of collage happens. Allow yourself to be open to possibility.

www.cos-ahmet.co.uk

1 *The Flower Portrait*, 2010. Mixed media collage, newspaper cutting of 'The Flower Portrait' of Shakespeare, black leather, silk chiffon obscure.
2 *Altered State III*, 2010. Self Portrait collage, manipulated using part images of *The Turin Shroud* and *Salvatore Mundi* after Da Vinci, including other found images and acetate.
Photographs ©: Cos Ahmet

1

2

3

4

BRONIA DANIELS

I love the tactile, versatile nature of fabrics and believe that art should be more than a simply visual experience. For this reason, I encourage people to touch my artworks, stepping past the usual 'look but don't touch' gallery policies. In my work I use vintage clothing, new fabrics, accessories and beads and contrasting patterns, colour and textures.

www.bdesigns.co.uk

1 *Untitled*. Fabric and buttons.
2 *Untitled*. Fabric and buttons.
3 *Untitled*. Fabric and buttons.
4 *Untitled*. Fabric and buttons.
Photographs ©: Bronia Daniels

EMILY JO GIBBS

Having established an international reputation for her exquisite handbags, Emily Jo Gibbs has recently turned to textiles and thread to render portraits of her family. Emily has a wonderful talent for combining materials and creates beautiful objects that have been inspired by her observations of nature.

emilyjogibbs.co.uk

Billy, 2011. Fabric, appliqué and threads. Photograph ©: Michael Wicks

1

2

3

CATHERINE GREEN

I experiment with different forms of mark-making on fabric to create personal pieces. My work combines painterly brush strokes with crisp screen prints and utilizes everyday items, such as bubble wrap and plastic mesh, to create interesting effects.

catherinegreen.co.uk

1 *Climbing*, 2010. Dye, paint, silk viscose, satin, velvet devore and stitch. Photograph ©: Yvonne Grist
2 *Orange and Black*, 2010. Materials as for 1, above. Photograph ©: Catherine Green
3 *Wilderness* , 2010. Materials as for 1, above. Photograph ©: Yvonne Grist

SANDEEP JANDU

I developed these illustrations for my degree specialism in illustration. The brief was to design a book jacket for George Orwell's *1984*. The story deals with memories and experiences of hurt and loss and secrets. For this reason I chose subtle tones such as brown, gold and white, to create a sense of distance, loss and something antique.

1984 project, 2009. Paper collage and print.

1

2

CAROLINE KIRTON

My work is a series of snap shots of the ups and downs of teenage life, based on my observations of my daughters and their friends. It is an on-going study of my relationship with them and how it is always evolving. In my work I try to create a sense of autobiography, recording stories, feelings, emotions and moments in time.

carolinekirton.blogspot.com

1 *Alright Don't Cry About It.* Appliqué, machine embroidery and mixed media.
2 *My Mum's a Proper Weirdo!* Appliqué, machine embroidery and mixed media.
Photographs ©: Frame One Photography

1

2

3

MÄRTA MATTSSON

Sometimes I see beauty in things that other people find strange or are even repulsed by. I am fascinated by this reaction. My work deals with the tension that lies between attraction and repulsion. I use materials such as vellum, butterflies and silver, to give familiar objects an extraordinary and unfamiliar feel.

martamattsson.com

1 *Wing Necklace*, 2010. Vellum made from goat, butterflies, nylon thread. Photograph ©: Dominic Tschudin
2 *Bow brooch*, 2010. Vellum, nylon thread and silver. Photograph ©: Märta Mattsson
3 *Bow earring* , 2010. Vellum, nylon thread and silver. Photograph ©: Märta Mattsson

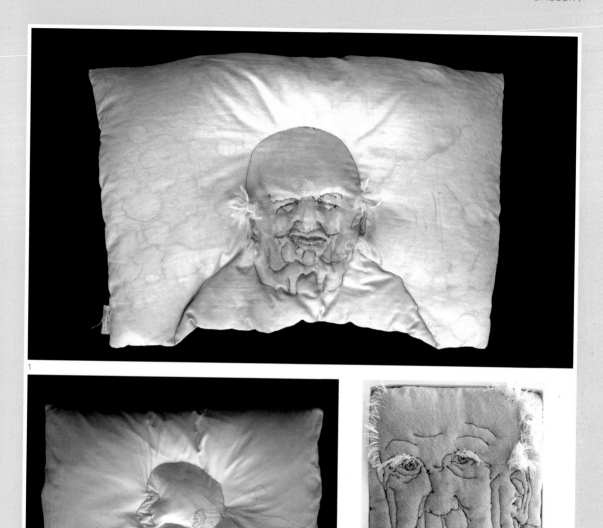

GEORGIE MEADOWS

My work is inspired by the people I have been working with as an Occupational Therapist; their bravery and their sense of having lost their identity. My advice to new mixed-media artists is to practice drawing the image you are going to use until you know it really well, then let the fabric, thread and the sewing machine have their influence on your work. It's OK to unpick!

1 *Man on Pillow*, 2005. Free machine stitch, fabric, wadding, fabric paint.
2 *Woman on Pillow*, 2007. Free machine stitch, fabric, wadding.
3 *Man in Plaster Frame*, 2005. Free machine stitch, fabric, wadding, fabric paint.
Photographs ©: Daniel Meadows

Fly away home
spread your wings and fly
Take the beauty of your soul
and share it with the sky

1

2

3

DEBBIE SMYTH

My aim is to explore thread as a drawing tool. I plot the drawing out first to give me the bare bones of the composition, and then gradually add more thread and knots, just as you would add shading with a pencil. Thread is a soft and pliable material that creates a wonderful quality of line.

debbiesmyth.blogspot.com

All images are from the *Fly Away Home* installation, created for the Stroud International Textile Festival, 2011. Fabric, dressmaking pins, thread and MDF.
Photographs ©: Zac Mead

1

2

3

4

JULIE VERMEILLE

Julie Vermille is a trained illustrator who bases her work in textiles and thread on drawings done in ink. She uses thread in her work, 'as a symbol of time, of relations between one space and another; closeness, tightness, as well as breakages and knots'. Fabric patterns are a significant source of inspiration and often lead to the floral and vegetal elements in her designs.

julievermeille.com

1 *Beautiful Coincidences series*, 2011.
2 *Woodland Creatures series*, 2011.
3 *Beautiful Coincidences series*, 2011.
4 *Beautiful Coincidences series*, 2011.
Materials for all: fabric, paper, fabric collage, ink.
Photographs ©: Julie Vermeille

Stockists

Try your local haberdashery, or the haberdashery section in your nearest department store. Local craft fairs and flea markets are also a good place to source material and objects that you may wish to use in your work.

Atlantis Arts
atlantisart.co.uk
+44 (0)20 7377 8855

Paperchase
paperchase.co.uk

The Japanese Paper Place
japanesepaperplace.com

Somic Textiles
somic.co.uk
+44 (0)1772 790 000

Fibre Crafts
georgeweil.com/Fibrecrafts
+44 (0)1483 565 800

John Lewis
johnlewis.com
+44 (0)8456 049 049

Specialist Crafts
specialistcrafts.co.uk
+44 (0)1162 697 711

Cass Art London
cassart.co.uk
+44 (0)20 7354 2999

Hobby Craft
hobbycraft.co.uk
+44 (0)845 051 6599

Johnson Crafts
johnsoncrafts.co.uk

Fred Aldous
fredaldous.co.uk
+44 (0)1612 364 224

Threads of Imagination
threadsofimagination.co.uk
+44 (0)1633 482 058

Home Crafts Direct
homecrafts.co.uk
+44 (0)1162 697 733

Index